NATIONAL GEOGRAPHIC

D0100646

People Who Lead Us

Lesley Pether

What is a leader?

A leader shows people how to do things.
Leaders help people work together as a team.

18

Mr. Young is a basketball coach.

Mr. Young teaches the
players how to play basketball.
He teaches players the rules of the game.
He also shows them how to play as a team.

NYSP

Mrs. Lin is the principal of a school.

Mrs. Lin works with the teachers in the school. She helps them get the materials they need. She also helps them work together as a team.

Parkdale School Roster
M T W T
9:00
10:00
11:00
12:00
1:00
2:00
3:00
4:00
Ms. SHANKS
Ms. LORENC
MR. BOLTON
Ms. LORENC
MR. GILLESPIE
Work Vehicles

Mr. Sampson is a scout troop leader.

Mr. Sampson shows the scouts how to put up tents.
He teaches the scouts how to build campfires.
He also teaches them to work together as a team.

Ms. Martino is an orchestra conductor.

Ms. Martino leads all the musicians in the orchestra. She tells the musicians how to play the music. She also helps them play together as a team.

Index

basketball coach 4–5

orchestra conductor 10–11

principal 6–7

scout troop leader 8–9